American Ephemeral

American Ephemeral

Poems by

Justin Hamm

Kelsay Books

Cover art: Justin Hamm

ISBN: 13-978-1-945752-73-5

Kelsay Books
Aldrich Press
www.kelsaybooks.com

Acknowledgments

Grateful acknowledgment is made to the editors of the following journals, in which some of these poems were first published, occasionally in a different version:

apt, Atticus Review, decomP, Common Ground Review, Escape into Life, Heavy Feather Review, Indianola Review, I-70 Review, The Lascaux Review, New Plains Review, Pittsburgh Poetry Review, REAL: Regarding Arts & Letters, Referential Magazine, Rust + Moth, San Pedro River Review, and *Stoneboat.*

A special thanks to Michael Meyerhofer for his friendly eye and encouraging words on this manuscript. And, as always, thanks to Mel and our babies for the love and for the time.

Contents

Worried Playground Daddy's Blues

On the playground I strum guitar while my daughter
dangles upside down from the bar above the tall slide,

and inside my middle-aged brain a movie
plays: the pop-art radiance of ambulance lights,

then the cold eye of a weary doctor who rubs
the bridge of his nose and glances back

at the darkly-cloaked hospital chaplain
before clearing his throat to speak.

Enough of that, I say. *I don't want you
to hurt yourself.* Trying to sound composed

when what I mean is *I love you please
don't die on me the way my mother did.*

Something about Missouri in November,
the trees so recently vacant of leaves.

That and another bad triglycerides reading
have me on high alert,

but then, I hear we've all gone half-insane
with protectiveness, and I believe it,

can remember how Mom let us roam freely
the trailer park and the thick woods,

how we skipped alongside passing Amtraks,
checking in only for Kool-Aid and ham sandwiches.

God, I wish I could go back, take her by the shoulders,
look her in the eyes and say *come on, just pay attention*,

not at all for those sweet dangers she permitted us
but because our time was already evaporating.

Oklahoma

Where grown-old pickups go
to live out their remaining days.
The rusty, the crusty, the boxlike in body,
the last of the clunker-cash refugees
parked outside of midcentury diners
or near the downest and dirtiest dives—
or else half off the highway, like this F-150,
the powdered blue one with the red dirt dusting her hood
and the red dirt grubbing up her wheelwells,
the same red dirt found on the bootsoles
of the grizzled old cowboy
who wakes in her cab and straightens his hat
and steps gingerly into the hot Oklahoma sun
to the sounds of bone creak and joint pop.
Who two-minute gravel coughs his lungs clear
and leans smoking against her tailgate
as he scans the red dirt horizon for signs
of the invisible pale horse rider.

Begin with a Whole Boy,

two sea green eyes, ten fingers, and a tangle of dark hair tossed over his forehead. A whole boy with a whole crush on a small girl wearing braces and a rock T-shirt from the early 1970s. Now throw in a drill press and another boy, one who may or may not also have a crush on the small girl. Observation would seem to suggest that she, at least, has a crush on him.

The whole boy pulls down on the drill press lever, shaping wheels en masse for the class's next project, CO_2 race cars for the school derby. He may be working the drill press, but he's watching his crush and her crush, and when the two pass in the center of the woodshop and the small girl hands off a note, the whole boy loses half his concentration. There is suddenly a great quantity of blood.

From somewhere inside the mess of blood a thumbnail corkscrews upward, a heap of mottled flesh, a bone that isn't meant to be seen without an X-ray. The whole boy does not seem to notice. In fact, it is only when the shop teacher chokes out a very bad word and wraps the ruined thumb in his paisley necktie that the whole boy finally glances away from the middle of the room, eyes blinking rapidly in confusion.

In some ways, it isn't nearly as bad as it could be. At the hospital the whole boy and his parents learn every part is still in place, that the scars will eventually heal. He nods as each grown person reminds him just how lucky he is not to have lost a thumb that day, or worse. He nods and he seems to agree. Sometimes he even repeats that last word back to the speaker: "Worse." But in truth his mind has never left the woodshop. His mind's eye has never stopped staring into its terrible, tainted center. And in that moment there is nothing anyone can say that will make him believe he can ever be whole again.

In Little League Once

after bobbling
a slow bouncer,
I made the mistake
of rolling my eyes
at our coach,
who grabbed my collar
and hissed
his terrible coffee
breath
into my pale face
until I began
to sob and jerk
like a puppet.

When he let go
and turned back
toward
the dugout,
he was forced
to look up
and then
look up again
just to meet
the hard eyes
of the man
whose right hand
had just grabbed
ahold
of his collar.

Hell, I don't
know why

I even told you
that story just now.
I don't condone
collar grabbing,
would prefer
nobody ever grab
anybody's collar
much less do
whatever
comes after that.

I guess part
of me just wishes
every little boy
had one chance
to see his old man
that way.

First Lesson in Meat, 1984

They crash through
the ratty screen door,
all gunflash and colorful
beer cans.
Five men, blood or in-law,
their patchy-bearded
throats alive
with hunter laughter
and gruff guy chatter.
Up front, my grandfather
Undisputed chief, he holds
the pink thing, the dead
rabbit-flesh thing,
one ear in each of his hands.

These were hands that held me
in my towel after a bath,
comforted me writhing
and screaming at dream demons
in the deepest cricket hours
of the night.
Hands that poured
my milk,
chocolate or white,
and parted my translucent hair,
and tied and delicately retied
my shoelaces after my mother
forbid me Velcro.

These were hands that often
rested so tenderly against
my cheek—

and still they could kill
and cut and rip
the skin from what they'd slayed.
And before they'd even seen
a sink of soapy water,
they would reach out to hold
me again—
still my grandfather's hands
but changed now,
somehow different.
Streaked in pink, washed.
But only in the blood
of their own making.

Rapid Refund

In the buy-everything supermarket lot, the wild-eyed angel-child, the one all the teachers pity and call *princess poverty,* her tiny face a dream of joy and concentration, her tiny feet pumping furiously those brand-new-bike pedals as if she might pedal herself into some other universe entirely—one where the daddies get parole, or don't, if they're the hurting kind, and nobody has to pack up and move when it's still dark out, and the mommies don't have half so many bruises or boyfriends. And sure, maybe yesterday such an idea would've just seemed little-kid stupid, but today, see, today is tax refund day when the sun smiles down like a coloring book sun and the tulips and peach blossoms seem to boogie to the beep of her brassy bicycle horn. All things on earth and in heaven are possible on tax refund day. Even a universe in which the car salesmen and funeral directors have but one smile apiece, and fewer pockets.

If Only Ken Burns

could get his hands on this footage. Telemachus,
aged eight years, already thickening, athletic
but still uncertain in his movements. The big neighborhood
ballgame against the brutes who would become
known forever as suitors. Third inning,
towering popup to left. T. calls for it
the whole way, but Odysseus snares it barehanded
just inches above the boy's outstretched glove.
Not hard to see how such a move might confirm,
I don't really trust you, son. A boy may spit
into the dirt for consolation, rub at it with his cleated sandal,
but these are the moments that burrow deep,
that fester, only to surface once the boy becomes
a man, armed with a ninety-plus per hour sinker
that dives like a trained falcon—a gift he honed alone
chucking rocks against rocky hillsides during long
and fatherless summers beneath the white Ithacan sun.

Odysseus. Broken king. PTSD. Bone-heavy, slower now
of wit and reflex, already an hour or two deep
into his cups. Does he understand his son's words
carry more of a threat now than an entreaty?
In his hands the prince holds two weather-beaten
lumps of broken cowleather. *Hey, Pops,* he says,
what say you and me have a quick game of catch?
And he holds the gloves out, not quite in offering.

Barn Jamboree, Rosine, Kentucky

Sunset slants its salmon light
through the open doors.
A man, whom we're told
has recently (and only just barely)
survived the bypassing
of multiple arterial blockages
by a hotshot surgeon
down in Bowling Green,
accepts a battered house Martin,
takes the stage to perform here
for the first time in many months.

He adjusts the microphone,
toys with the tuners,
glances around the twilit barn nervously,
finally nodding at the audience
seated on long benches like church pews.
But before he can begin
a lovely woman about his age
sidles up from the side, surprising him.
She gives him a look that seems to ask
if there's any chance of a duet,
and you don't have to be local
to work out that there's been
some history between them.

Enough so that when he picks
out the first notes
and begins to strum "Waltz Across Texas,"
their voices entwine, naturally,
like the fingers of the old
couples who stand and press close

and sway together
only a little more carefully
than they must have fifty-odd years ago
when this song and their love
were both newborn to the world.

Joy is a complicated matter;
it almost never arrives crystalline.
I have seen it bloom
even on the faces of broken men
buying cheap beer on the odd
Tuesday in November,
unmistakable but muddied up always,
mixed with a hint of guilt or resignation.
The singing man's face is like that.
So is the lady's.
You can see they are doing something
they once believed
they might never do again
and now must consider
what other dreamghosts
they might yet sing life into.

The tune is like any other tune,
and soon enough it shuffles toward an end.
But her fingers find his shoulder,
and a silent conspiracy ensues
to strum on and reprise the chorus
once, and then twice more,
as if they are terribly afraid
for the sound to stop,
afraid to step out from behind
the sweet safety of perhaps.
And then they must, and do.

The bow, the wave, the decision:
all arrive together in an instant.
She leaves him with a kiss on the cheek
that brings high color to his face,
floats out with the applause
into the soft Kentucky twilight.

The rest of the evening he can be seen
slouching, exhausted, near the back
entrance to the barn
as the regular band swings, western-style.
Every so often he runs his hand
absently over the area of his chest
where beneath his plaid shirt I imagine
must live one hell of a scar
from all this business with his heart.

First Lesson in Ephemerality

My grandfather bought his burial plot early,
tucked away in a small country cemetery
adjacent to a sturdy old corn-and-cows farm.

From his chosen spot, the soft green hills
rolled off toward a far horizon, and beyond
that a mysterious land in which he believed

he'd someday live, perhaps even settle
unless the sum deeds of his life meant
the final judgement went another way.

But he must have thought too of the shell
he'd be leaving behind, laid up under
all that heartland sod and soil indefinitely,

since he'd planted a tree like those found
back in his native Kentucky so that he might
rest again in the shade he'd loved as a boy.

This weekend we watched thirty-year-old
home VHS tapes, all the people in them now dead
in one sense or another, though some sat

right next to me on the sofa as the video
wobbled and blinked in and out, going dark
and fuzzy every fifteen or twenty seconds.

I don't mean this critically. We all die
a number of times before we cease biologically,
each change a small stepping-stone death

on the way up to the big dark leap into the empty;
even this poem will have died many times
before meeting your critical or sympathetic eye.

On these home movies I heard my grandfather's voice
before it had gone rough and world-weary,
before the slow death of its youth and vigor.

In one tape, he narrated a walk through his garden,
in the next he sang old Carter Family songs,
in a third he called out, teasing his eldest, my mother.

My mother's grave is near to my grandfather's.
On her headstone, my father's name, the dates
marking his lifespan already half carved, waiting.

Dad says he regrets having it made this way, and me
I suppose I regret my crimes against the spirit
of what I purport to stand for, believe in.

Our regrets are most resistant to small deaths;
they habitate in us like household ghosts
until our houses finally burn down or collapse.

Listen: here I wanted to return you to the cemetery,
to tell you something about the breeze there
on certain warm afternoons, but I just can't

seem to stop touching everything around me—
memorizing all matter as it exists on this particular day
through fingertips, through palms or cheeks.

Here's an orange. Here is a guitar. Here, my father's
big shoulders. This is my daughter's tiny hand.
This: a book. These: the soft hairs on my wife's neck.
And this: today's fleeting version of my face.

The Farmers at Their Morning Coffee

Hear what news passes their lips
between the slow, ginger sips
from steaming plastic cups
at the local Hardee's.

Hear the coded odes
to past courting prowess,
the ballads of Mesozoic-like fish
caught not by pole but old-fashioned
Lincoln-style wrestling.

Uniformed in shirtsleeves
and meshback feedcompany hats,
they tell of coon dogs
treeing iguanas, old flood stories
to rival Gilgamesh or the Bible.

They tell in hushed voices
of witchwives who watch and hear
from afar the truth of a man's heart.

Was another pitiful year
for the crops, says one.
Too wet to plant in the spring
and too dry to grow
in the summer, says another.
This one's circulatory piping
has clogged up again.

And now the cold, too, has returned.
They all agree it really is
the deep kind that settles

into earth and old bones alike.
Things are always just a little
bit worse than they were
this time yesterday morning.

Still, it must feel good to be
so old and alive on this frosty morning,
to drink such hot coffee
and perhaps pick over
a rubbery breakfast platter
while curing the literal truth
of its shameful lack of color
here at this table where all the seats
are filled for only God
knows how much longer.

Arthur and Marie, 1961

Late autumn now, Illinois. The trees, half-dead,
wave their gnarled arms above the bone
white gravel of the rural country road

down which he steers the old rustbucket flatbed,
her nose toward the pinkish twilight, toward a town
where they'll meet his folks for supper.

The day has been a long one, full of harsh fieldwork
and minor disagreements that kept them from sharing
they've both been dreaming of a child again.

Now he is sorry and she is ready to let him be,
and so his hand bridges their space, finding her cheek
for a sweet second before shooting back to the wheel.

At the far reach of their headlights, a great ghostlike bird—
a snowy owl, perhaps, though rare around here.
It sits in stony stillness between the drying cornfields.

Consider the intricacies of human recollection.
If she is, in fact, with child, they will one day turn
this vision into an omen, even making an angel

of its wide white wings and its sudden skyward ascension,
everything electric with importance—their shallow breath
as they watch, eyes wide and unblinking, the way

their hands find each other and interlock on her knee.
Just as true is the opposite—the bird becomes the angel
of death if what's stirs in her is instead malignant.

But if she is empty, except for her basic dissatisfaction,
then the vision astonishes only for that brief instant.
Once it is gone, it is, truly and finally, gone.

In fact, trees, road, twilight, autumn, corn: all gone,
the whole scene blended into the dense camouflage
of memory, forgotten fifteen years, then twenty more,

until even that cells-deep desire for a child of their flesh
is lost to them, buried beneath her kindly cynicism,
barred behind his stoic, even-if-my-back's-broke will.

Forgotten so long it is left, finally, to the storyteller's invention.
Buried so deep when the dust is finally blown off
they can only imagine it a fiction that never existed at all.

Farmer, Clutching Chest

The circumstance of his death is nigh.
But as luck would have it, this tragedy
is not without heart; it has gone out ahead
to build an afterlife for him.
Now it stands, silhouetted against a far sunset,
arms raised, waving. The farmer can't see
that far but he imagines his death is smiling.
It wants to know if this is the right place,
this sad plot that seems so much like the harsh
lands he'll soon be leaving.
Yes, he nods, *that's the place*. He can hardly wait.
He wants to gather all that good soil
in his fingers, to horde it to himself.
He wants all of it: the inelegance of pig stench
and the garble of good tires treading on gravel road.
Doesn't he understand it will be hard?
He understands, wants it that way. Is he supposed to
ask for some sort of hoity-toity heaven?
Hell, that's all he's ever known is survival,
and he must know if he can do it there, too—
in the afterlife, where the cruel wind draws itself
from old testament sources,
and where the unimaginable drought of eternity
will press constantly against the green edges
of all he dares to grow.

Old Men Laughing on a Park Bench in Early October

One grips the iron armrest; the other clutches a fedora from a distant past. Both shake and shake and shake. Their eyes stretch wide. The inner wells from which they draw their joy must be deeper than any I've witnessed in my short life. Watching, I forget for a moment the reason I am even sitting here, and who I believe is to blame. The three of us, and the dew glittering diamondlike on the grass, and the first few vibrant leaves of fall—for a moment we don't seem to belong to the world of solid things. But eventually, the laughter does sputter to a stop, and the silence in its wake is so heavy and total by contrast, it is like a preview of the great long silence to come. Perhaps the old men recognize this, too, because after a minute, one of them—the one with the fedora—grins, shakes his head slowly and repeats the inciting word again: *curtains.* But of course: nothing this time, no reaction from either of them. The moment's magic is all used up. It is right about then that I look over my shoulder and discover my bad news tromping through the grass. He holds his head high and I can hear him whistling his lonesome train-whistle whistle as he approaches, a violent whistle, a whistle that rips through the laughter-less quiet without conscience. I am on the tracks, and I think to myself, *What can I do, what, honestly, can I do, but rise and turn my face and wait to meet whatever may be coming?*

First Lesson in Vietnam, 1987

It was how you stood on your trailer roof
all that sweltering Independence Day, caped
in a threadbare flag of our nation, encircled
by Budweiser empties, plates of burning incense.
It was how you stood there and also how,
lit from above by those colorful celebration
bombs, you made me believe in the myth
of the romantic savage. I had no idea then
what you'd tried to accomplish alone
in the toolshed with the extension cord,
nor how, in a few years, you'd be hauled in—
armed robbery, just days after the first
Gulf War broke out. I saw only your hair,
shoulder length, and your scarred torso
bare and bony, home to a tattooed menagerie
of fantasy creatures: elf, dragon, phoenix,
centaur, faerie, citizens of a land
to which you'd gladly defect. It was all that,
and it was how recklessly you lit
bottle rockets and fired them from your
hollowed-out walking stick. And it was how—
finally—when my father cupped his hands together
and shouted, *Hey, Chuck, give it a rest, guy.*
It's getting pretty late, you turned, delicate
as a dancer in the shimmering moonlight,
and offered him what little was left
of your mangled middle finger.

Days Like This

Mama told me there would be
a great battle called Ragnarok,
that I would be its lone survivor.

She told me the sharp way
I tied my shoelaces
would cause lovely women
to swoon.

She said my above-average IQ
would summons
a robed flock of adoring Magi
to the foot of my bed.

Mama told me cornbread
would turn my muscles into pulleys,
that I could beat that steel-
driving machine
with the sheer force of my charm.

She told me twelve times six
was whatever I wanted it to be,
that I had the kind of power
to transcend silly mathematics.

She said my singing voice
could revive a slaughtered longhorn,
that I need not go to church
for God was already seeking me.

My mama was a talker, and she
said so many things,

but unlike the wise matriarch
of the Shirelles song,
she never once informed me
there'd be days like this.

And so imagine my surprise
as I stand here on the banks
of a wild, imaginary river
I have invented only for
the sake of metaphor.

Imagine me jumping in,
believing I will swim.

Imagine me not swimming.

Imagine me swept downstream,
deeply panicked, eyes like a pair
of electrocuted olives—
or else some better image
if you can think of one
since you are the one imagining.

What I'm saying is, imagine
my deep, unholy surprise at learning
that despite what Mama said
I cannot in fact breathe
under water.

Imagine my shock upon realizing
days like this do indeed exist.

I Take Forty-Five Minutes to Shoot a Portrait
of My Father

My father standing here
now leaning over there
now turning his patient face
first left and then right.

Tilting his bearded chin
according to my instruction.

Grinning at an old joke
I've raked up from our past
to crinkle his eyes
and soften his expression.

This posing is real work for him
but no complaints—
the old man is of a certain generation
and he understands effort
as a brand of broad currency
that can mean good faith
to business partners or employers
and to a lover can mean
that long-awaited shedding
of the selfishness
that shells us all in our youth.

Here it means a mere portrait
can transform into the words
I want but fail to speak.

Weeks later, when I finally
give him this print
matted and framed in barnwood
I will give to him himself
precisely the way I see him.

And the effort spent will read
like a personal inscription
scrawled not onto the back
of the photograph itself
as might be the custom
but directly into the soft meat
that makes my father's heart.

Playing Blues Harp Alone in an Unfinished Basement

At a ballgame once,
I saw a great hero
with comic book biceps
launch three home runs
of gargantuan distance.
He circled the bases
more slowly each time,
as if perhaps he grasped
just how fleeting
his greatness would be—
but no, I believe he meant
to embarrass the pitcher,
a renowned and arrogant
goateed villain
who liked to fill
the daily news with
the legend of himself.

That hero fell, of course,
and to such depths
that a common stooge
such as myself
can now feel justified
in pitying him—
and I do pity him,
not for losing greatness
but for having ever
borne it at all.
You see, once a person
has reached the pinnacle,
he can never again

find any real pleasure
in being well and truly inept.

I'm glad there's
no chance I'll ever
ascend to greatness.
I prefer to know
how sweet it feels
on a stray Saturday
in late April, let's say,
the wife and the baby
off in town, visiting,
plenty of cold beers
stacked in the fridge,
to toss the drywall knife
on top of the unopened
bucket of joint compound
and drop the needle
on Howlin' Wolf instead.

I know we're not supposed
to admit such scandals,
but every now and again
I *like* to be reminded
most of what we do
doesn't really matter.
I like that I can
simply close my eyes
and blow along
with boozy conviction
and even see the humor
a few minutes later

when I discover my
suppose'd best friend
and confidant the dog
has once again buried
her head deep in the laundry
piled in the corner.

Late August

All that summer the trailer park baked beneath the cruelest sun in recent memory. A drought year. The slender grass strips serving as backyards yellowed before slowly achieving a pale brown color, a texture strawlike and crunchy underfoot. Where grass would not grow the dry dirt cracked and ant armies crawled in long black trains up from the jagged gaps, scouting out dropped popsicles, discarded hot dogs, open trash containers.

Everywhere was heard the rumbling hum of window AC units, of laughing children, dirt-faced, tongues Kool-Aid red, small bellies full of cold ham sandwich. Here and there sat the elderly streetside in woven lawn chairs or on yard swings, sipping golden sweet tea. Against the logic of the heat they wore long pants and sleeves and did not sweat.

In other driveways shirtless men hunched over the engines of rusted jalopies, barking long curse strings as if to invoke the secret language of automobile resurrection. Their blue, gylphlike tattoos hid in the shade of the car hoods but revealed their mysterious selves when the men stood upright and lit cigarettes and rolled their shoulders and leaned far forward and then far backward to stretch stiff muscles while contemplating the dysfunction hidden within the guts of these machines.

Someone somewhere on this street or the next cooked meat over a charcoal flame, or so smell would indicate. A boy stood atop a dumpster at the head of the road, face tilted upward to the sun as he drained a bottle of orange soda in four or five loud gulps. The trailers themselves with their faded paint, with their shades liked closed eyelids, appeared ill or even passed out sleeping. Five or six weeks rolled on, days and nights identical in their slow-spinning relentlessness.

48

One afternoon, a fat purple storm cloud approached but blew by without relinquishing a single raindrop. The tease of it must have been too much. That afternoon, two neighbors, the war veteran and the carpenter, altercated over borrowed money, prescription pills, a woman they both believed they could own. But it turns out they were mistaken. A knife blade appeared, mirroring back the white daylight. There came an animal grunt. Later, near where her car had been parked, the dark stain on the gravel driveway told another chapter of the story.

The Man in Line at the Grocery Store in Centralia, Missouri

has a face like a confession.

It says, I have come here to buy cheap bread
and milk for this herd of children
you see crammed into my cart.

It says, I am happy to have these children
whose dirty faces and empty bellies
give my life a kind of worth.

It says, My patience is not
what it used to be, but I try.

It says, I broke a promise once,
a clean bright golden nugget
of a promise, and instead
of two neat half-promises
that might someday reunite,
this promise crumbled into
a fine and wispy dust.

It says, It gets pretty windy here
in the flatter parts of Missouri.

It says, Yes, there was a woman, once—
now darkens, says, Of this, I will say no more.

It says, I am astonished at the joy
I find through my children,
but a man's heart, full as it might be,
can still dream the hobo's dream

of rails and railcars, or of a tiny
homestead and fealty to none
but its own shifting jurisdiction.

It says, Such a heart can still dream
itself a dirt path that winds down
and further down to the cold river
where fleshpeople can go and make
acquaintance with the ghosts.

But, it says, we need always remember—
the ghosts themselves must be willing.

Carrying Home the Feast

Hard, even now, to recall the shame of it:
the annual grocery sack stuffed near to bursting
with nonperishables, gifts from gooey-hearted
room mothers, their eyes wet messes of matted mascara
from the sight of your thriftstore corduroys
and the crooked frames of your state-bought glasses.

Canned corn, cranberry sauce, boxed potato flakes
and pre-packaged stuffing—here was every necessity
for your thirty-minute Thanksgiving feast.
But any bag big enough to fill a family of four
draws unwanted attention on a school bus full
of high-dollar, question-marked jeans and sneakers
with futuristic air pumps built into the tongues.
Plus, it occupies the entire seat beside you—
a spot where, hypothetically at least, a friend might sit.

You were eleven the year you finally decided
the embarrassment was too much.
A first, misguided, act of rebellion,
but how light the walk down the bus aisle
and home through the streets of the trailer park
that late November afternoon
without the dreaded cargo you'd left
half-leaning against the flagpole at dismissal.
How quiet too the usual voices of ridicule
who already lived like malevolent tree elves
in the hollows of your adolescent mind.

And how impossibly short-lived your escape.
As soon as you stepped, empty-handed,
into the wood-paneled kitchen where your mother

sat smoking in her work apron, you transformed.
No longer her little boy, you were just
another man in the long, crooked train
of cowardly men who eventually let her down.

Marriage (Detail)

She wakes me unexpectedly
in the dead of the night,
panicked, breathing hard,
asking, "Is she talking to me,
is she talking to me?"

"Who?" I say.

"The doll," she says. "The *doll*."
Then immediately begins
to snore again, leaving me alone
to contemplate that
while staring into the darkness.

Children in the Middle Ages

Earlier that night, a middle-aged man dressed himself in a cape and green tights and shimmied up a tree to rescue his neighbor's new kitten. We sat numbly over our steaming hamburger pie, watching first the climbing oil prices and then the live feed as our would-be hero lay in a twisted heap on the sidewalk at the base of the tree, his neck in fifty shattered pieces, blood fleeing his faulty skull in astonishing haste. In the dining room, us, meaning: you, me, and the sick child whose cough occasionally ripped across the newscaster's flat Midwestern cadence. After dinner, you were supposed to be reading her a book about children in the middle ages, the games they played, but you kept looking up at the television. This was not a good time in our marriage, though it was perhaps a little better a time than now, at least. I don't suppose you remember how you turned, or how we looked at one another for a handful of seconds? I thought we were speaking to each other without words, a secret language of understanding. You thought I was being weird. Eventually, one of us must have found the remote and changed the channel. Or maybe we just turned the TV off. That is where the silence begins in my memory, and I have yet to come to the other side of it. It is a sound so loud and terrible, I'm not even sure you can hear me trying to tell you this now.

First Morning in the Mountains

The day before, remember,
had been that special
travel chaos
families must endure.

But now, all of us
fully rested
from the long road trip,
we couldn't stop
grinning.

Outside, the bears
foraged beneath
a golden sunrise.

Inside the chilly cabin
you held our baby girl
babbling on your hip
and warmed the skillet,
lobbing the occasional
happy thought
into the living room
as you felt inclined.

Beneath a blanket
on the sofa
our older daughter and I
reworked
every pop song we knew
to reference bacon.

How is it there are
no pictures to post,
not a single selfie
to crop or filter?

Surely the camera battery
must have been dead,
our cell phones
mislaid for the moment.

Or else—no.
I think maybe it was
just that good.
I think we must have
felt so alive
in that moment,
so entirely ourselves,
neither of us could bear
to pause
for the time it would take
to tame and frame
the glorious freedom
burning from our faces

Museum Guard's Blues

There was this old man and he always wore a blues player's fedora, just like the one I liked to wear. He would cry in front of the romantic landscapes in a way that made you want to hold his hand. The walls and the ceiling were transparent. Outside, you could see when thunderstorms gathered with menacing intent.

The president at this time was a person history would not remember with kindness. A know-it-all woman stood in a shadowy corner, passing on spurious information about the French and Indian War. There were dozens of mournful sculptures from different historical eras. To me they all seemed to be wailing in a single voice. I had something like thirty dollars in my bank account and I was crazy in love with a performance artist who played classical music badly on purpose. I didn't get it and she refused to explain.

Sometimes I would look down at my own fingers in the cloudy dishwater or resting in my lap and they would seem to me the most foreign objects. They were capable of doing things, even if I was not. I would pick up the guitar and they would find the chords even when my mouth could not find the words. My fingers never seemed to care. They were of their own mind.

I had a child somewhere back there in my past but his mother put him up for adoption. I believe she would have made a damn good mother. I'd lived in three states in the past year alone but none of them had felt anything like a final destination. I have to wonder about people who think they have it all figured out and will even tell lies about the French and Indian War just to prove it to their own fearful hearts. This museum had once been my place of refuge. Now it just made me think about the history of my own misdeeds. I could see that the paintings hung along the walls were just a long, pretty documentation of an eternity of lies. I knew nobody would ever remember me after I was gone. It was a comfort to think this way.

I wanted to quit picking the guitar, to let my fingernails grow long and twisted like this man whose picture I'd seen once in a book. I wanted to do a kindness for someone and watch from a distance as she felt grateful toward a stranger. My father once told me the real measure of a man is his ability to grant forgiveness for all things. I wanted to believe that. Especially since my nose has always been a little crooked on my face because of him.

Three Days Driving Through Scrubby Desert and Semi-Arid Mountain,

ducking the stern southwestern sun within the walls
of ancient adobe missions Socorro County north.
Today, a church somewhere on the high road to Taos—
my seven-year-old daughter's patience for quiet places
breaks down entirely. She bounces from teal
flip-flop to teal flip-flop, whining she's *tired of Jesus
dying all over everywhere like this.*

At the mention of Jesus the three-year-old begins
to drum her Tinkerbell-shirted belly.
Hey, Daddy, Daddy, she wants to know, *was Jesus tough?
Well, well, well, did he have magic powers?*
And now the clouds empty.
Do Native Americans believe how Muslims believe? asks the eldest.
Did Jesus die 'cause he was mad at God? wonders the younger.

And so on. My wife and I take turns answering as best we can,
suddenly aware of the misunderstandings
our tiny, Midwest-cornfield existence has already weaved
into their worldview. While they process
all the new information, I study this ancient sanctuary,
adorned with solemn, staring statuettes, consider each
cruel station of the cross, nearly in tears trying to reconcile
the tremendous awe I always feel in houses of God
even twenty years after quitting my childhood church
over a dinosaur dispute
with the probability this mission was a factory of forced faith.

And then one more question cuts into my consciousness—
Daddy, are we *Christians?* Followed by the sound

of the mission doors swinging softly shut.
I breathe in. Look up at the wooden Mother and around
at a few other pilgrims who have wandered in behind us.
Even she, even they seem to be leaning forward,
leading with cupped ears, eager to know my answer.

First Lesson in The Dead

The Museum of International Folk Art, Santa Fe, NM

Wide blue sombrero haloing
        grim and fleshless grin

while slim skeleton fingers
        survey fret and string.

Across the wide aisle
        carved angels ascend

like *mariposas*, like butterflies,
        on pretty painted wings.

My preschool daughter
        simply does not care,

only moves her ear
        closer, as if trying to hear

what words the tiny
        bone man sings.

Pay Phones in the Underworld

My best friend texts me
a picture of a letter my mother
sent him the year she died.
He had forgotten about it
and wants to know whether
I want it for myself?

But the power isn't so much
in the ownership.
It arises from the surprise
in seeing the long loops
of her letters unexpectedly,
how they seem to carry
the very sound of her voice.

The dead know these things.
At just the right moment
they leave off from doing
their secret dead doings
and find a payphone, fish around
for change deep in the pockets
of their burial suits.

The call comes through
and on this end I pass a Camaro
just like the one Mom
rose hell with when we were kids.
Or the V.C. Andrews novels
stacked at the community yard sale
resurrect in my mind the rhythm
of her breathing as she read
evenings by yellow lamplight
in our smoky trailer.

But it's no use calling them.
The dead almost never answer.
You only tie up the line
as they stand patiently by,
tapping bony fingers to skulls
and waiting for the ringing to stop
so they know for certain the need
for reminder has ripened.

About the Author

Originally from the flatlands of central Illinois, Justin Hamm now lives near Twain territory in Missouri. He is the founding editor of *the museum of americana,* and his poems, stories, photos, and reviews have appeared in numerous publications, including *Nimrod, The Midwest Quarterly, Cream City Review,* and *Sugar House Review.* Recent work has also been selected for *New Poetry from the Midwest* (2014, New American Press) and the Stanley Hanks Memorial Poetry Prize from the St. Louis Poetry Center. His first collection, *Lessons in Ruin,* is also available from Aldrich Press/Kelsay Books.